AF334118

THE XYZ's OF BUSINESS WRITING

THE XYZ's OF BUSINESS WRITING

Sophisticated Concepts Made Simple

David G. Lyon

Dembner Books · New York

Dembner Books
Published by Red Dembner Enterprises Corp., 80 Eighth
Avenue New York, N.Y. 10011
Distributed by W. W. Norton & Company, Inc., 500 Fifth
Avenue, New York, N.Y. 10110

Library of Congress Cataloging in Publication Data

Lyon, David G. (David Gordon), 1911–
    The XYZ's of business writing.

    1. English language—Rhetoric. 2. English language
—Business English. 3. Technical writing. I. Title.
PE1479.B87L9 1986   808'.066651   85-25291
ISBN 0-934878-73-0
ISBN 0-934878-74-9 (pbk.)

Designed by Antler & Baldwin, Inc.

CONTENTS

Introduction

STRATEGY

TACTICS

INTRODUCTION

When Yogi Berra joined the Yankees as a rookie catcher, he told the training camp reporters, "Bill Dickey is learning me his experience."

That is what I have tried to do in this book—to distill for you the things I have learned in a lifetime of writing for business. Not the kind of ABC stuff Yogi Berra would have found in his how to catch guide, but the things he learned in years of major league competition.

I have divided the book into two main headings—strategy and tactics.

Strategy is the art of setting the right goals.

Tactics is the art of using the right methods to reach those goals.

What you write is strategy.

How you write it is tactics.

In any given situation there is usually *one* right strategy. I will show you the things you ought to evaluate in finding that strategy.

To carry out your strategy, there are usually dozens of right tactics—but thousands of wrong ones. I will help you find one of the tactics appropriate to your strategy.

I will be dealing with general principles that apply across the full range of business writing from short letters, memos, and directives to major reports, proposals, and plans. Principles that even apply to the writing of books—including this one.

This book is called the *XYZ's of Business Writing* because it is addressed to intelligent, successful people who are better at other things than they are at writing. In particular it should be helpful to thing oriented people—engineers, scientists, technicians, and supervisors—who don't feel particularly at home in the world of words, but who recognize the need for writing aptitude to advance their projects, their ideas, and their careers.

STRATEGY

I. UNDERSTANDING YOUR AUDIENCE

The first and most important step in writing is to understand who you're writing to—who they are and what they want.

To illustrate this point, let's turn the focus directly on *you*.

You are my audience. What do I know about you and how does it affect what I write and how I write it?

A. You are probably overloaded with work. You have a lot more on your mind than the need to improve your writing. So if I want your attention, I had better come to the point quickly.

B. You are bright, otherwise you would not have achieved the level where you must write important letters, reports, directives, proposals. This has a couple of consequences for me.

    1. I am not going to insult your intelligence with baby talk.

    2. I am going to try to stretch your mind with facts and ideas you may never have thought about, with confidence that anything I can pitch you can catch.

C. I know you no longer believe everything you read in books or hear in seminars. You look for credentials. So I am going to make a believer out of you. I can't just *tell* you what to do. I've got to show you that I know how to do it.

So in writing this I have got to do more than *give* examples. I have got to *be* an example.

Your writing skills probably are not up to the level of your other skills. And if so, they are standing in the way of your personal advancement and usefulness to your company.

One reason may be that you are addicted to fancy-pants writing, to calling a spade a portable manually operated agricultural implement. So it is not enough for me to tell you that simple, straightforward language is more effective. I must show you how to do it. This consideration has governed the way this book is written, not only the words, but the tone of voice.

To summarize, the way I write this book is shaped by my *total* perception of its readers—who you are, how you live and work, what you want and need, and what you will respond to. Similarly, what you write and how you write it must be shaped by a total understanding of your audience—their feelings, their functions, their needs—that goes below the surface of cliches and deals with things as they really are.

Basically, in business you have three kinds of written communication—those that go up, down, or sideways.

1. Upward-bound communications go to anybody who has power over you—your boss, his or her boss, any external regulating authority. You write to them about what you have done, plan to do, or want to do. You tell them enough so that they can feel comfortable about leaving you alone to handle the jobs or about giving you what you need to carry out your plans.

   To write effectively, you have to develop an understanding of management's whole system of priorities: their goals, their culture, their business environment, the language they feel comfortable with, the amount of detail they want, the stance they feel is appropriate for someone in your position. You may be writing to somebody who has an area of special interest and expertise, e.g., finance, engineering, sales, distribution, advertising, marketing, or R & D. You may be writing to an executive who has an overview of all functions, or (most difficult of all) your document may be going both to specialists and generalists. In all cases, you have to be aware of the interest of whatever audience you are writing to. *But whenever in doubt, write for the generalist*—for the person who is interested in the big picture.

2. When you are writing a communication directed downward, to anybody over whom you have power, you have to start out by asking yourself the same kind of questions. Naturally you get a very different set of answers.

You will probably find that people over whom you have power want to know the answers to questions such as:

"What do I have to do to please and satisfy you?"

"As of today, where do I stand with you?"

"If I do what you tell me to, what is in it for me?"

"What will happen if I fail?"

"What problems am I likely to run into?"

"Where do I turn for help if I need it?"

None of these questions, of course, arise when you are writing an upwardly directed communication.

Once you have really thought through your upward and downward relationships, you should not have to think them through again with every communication you write. Just be sure that you are really responding to what your recipient actually wants to know.

3. If you are writing a sideways communication, it is doubly important to be sensitive to the needs and attitudes of the recipient. Because no power flows in either direction, you must rely on persuasion. To motivate

your reader, you must really understand your reader's motivations, and that means going behind the textbook cliches to your reader's unexpressed thoughts and feelings. You must dig for the id.

For instance, whenever you try to sell a new product or idea, you encounter the unuttered but always present question:

> "Never mind the company, what's in it for me?"

On reflection it is naive to assume that your readers are solely motivated by what is best for their company—the lowest price, highest quality, fastest, most reliable service. Considerations such as these are means to an end, the advancement of your reader's own personal career objectives. If your reader believes that his company always recognizes and rewards the diligent pursuit of the company's best interests, these considerations alone will suffice. But, companies being what they are in this imperfect world, your reader in his secret self may be asking questions like these.

> "Why should I advance your proposal?"

> "If I quietly bury it, what's the risk?"

> "Can you go over my head or behind my back and make me look bad?"

"Whose toes do I step on if I accept your proposal?"

"Will you effect a noticeable improvement that will redound to my credit?"

"What are the chances that you can make a hero out of me, versus the chances you could make a bum out of me?"

"If something goes wrong, will you really stand behind me?"

"If this fails, who will my company blame—you or me?"

Questions such as these, because they are so rarely asked aloud, cannot be answered aloud. But they must be answered nevertheless.

Unless you are aware of these personal issues as well as the corporate issues, you may touch all the bases but fail to score.

In short in writing a sideways communication you must be street smart. You must ask yourself, "Am I writing to a coward? Who is my reader—a lion or a mouse?" If a lion, feed red meat. If a mouse, follow Groucho Marx's advice and throw down a piece of cheese.

For example, suppose your audience is a person (or persons) who fears that if they buy your proposition and something goes wrong all the blame will descend on them. You want them to feel that their boss and his boss knows your company well and favorably, and that it is not a reckless thing to accept your proposal. That becomes a communication objective. How do you attain it? Many ways. You might enclose samples of your company's advertising—copies of recent surveys, etc. The critical thing is to identify the need.

In writing a sideways communication to a stranger, your problem is complicated by the fact that they may think your letter is a piece of advertising mail and throw it away, unread. Computers and word processors have become so adept at simulating a personal letter that much genuinely personalized mail becomes suspect, and avoiding the wastebasket becomes your first overriding problem.

Recognizing that your prospective recipient is as snowed under by promotional mail as you are, saturated by the spurious, how can you hope your message will get through?

Nothing works all the time, but here are a few things I have found to be helpful.

a. Immediately I try to establish that this is a letter from a person, not a company. Example: If I were writing to rally-car fans, a mailing from the Chrysler Company would probably go directly into most wastebaskets unopened. A letter on Lee Iacocca's stationery would probably occasion a decent degree of interest among the unsophisticated. But a letter from Richard Roe, assistant to Lee Iacocca on rally-car design, would probably be target-specific. Having established that person-to-person atmosphere on the envelope, I would do my damndest to maintain it in the tone of voice throughout the letter. It would be me-Tarzan, you Jane—not me Chrysler, you customer.

b. As quickly as I can—in my very first sentence—I would establish promise of a basic benefit, strong enough and involving enough to make the reader want to learn more.

c. Before I did anything more to explain the benefit—to make it credible or desirable—I would establish a very strong sense of *urgency*. Get across the idea that time is limited, that it was not me but events and circumstances that were creating the pressure of time.

d. Then I would keep balancing the benefit factor with the urgency factor—concentrating on the benefit, but never letting the tension of urgency relax—until I had led the reader all the way down to and through the point of desired action.

The reason for maintaining this balance between benefit and urgency is that your letter is being read with tenuous attention. You are a self-interested intruder, not a welcomed guest. As long as you maintain the thrust of your argument in one direction, inertia works in your favor, and your recipient keeps on reading. But if you make a sudden swerve in the direction of your argument—e.g., from exposition of benefits to necessity for taking prompt decisions—your reader gets jolted off your train of thought and picks up the next letter. Your sale is gone.

II. DEFINING YOUR GOALS

If you cannot define your objectives, you will never achieve them.

Use the plainest, simplest terms. If you start using fancy, high-flown language, you will confuse or mislead yourself.

You should always be asking yourself two different kinds of questions:

1. What actions do I want to trigger?

   What am I trying to make happen?

2. What attitudes do I want to create?

   What am I communicating about me?

A. Triggering action—up, down, and sideways

1. If your communication is directed up, it may be your objective to:

Make sure they know

> what you have done
>
> what you are doing
>
> what you are planning

Get them to give

> you the okay
>
> the money
>
> the people you need

Assure them that everything is on target

Warn them of problems ahead

Urge them to take remedial or precautionary means

The list of possible objectives of an upwardly directed communication could go on and on, but the point to remember is: simplify your own definition of your goals to terms as plain as these.

2. Similarly if your communication is directed downward, its objective may be to:

Define exactly

> what you expect them to do
>
> how you want them to do it
>
> who they report to
>
> what are the ground rules

If you cannot reduce your message to simple terms, you should not expect your readers to be able to do it for you. It is their job to read your writing, not to read your mind.

3. When directing sideways communication, persuasion has to take the place of power. It is then that we most often fail to think clearly about the real world objective we are trying to achieve.

> **Example:** A salesperson is writing me. He wants to set up a date to see me. But instead of concentrating on the benefit an interview would have for me, he drifts off into extolling the product he is going to try to sell me.
>
> Instead of trying to open the door he is trying to close the sale.

It is hard enough to achieve a single objective when you are functioning within the framework of a power relationship. Once you step outside that framework into the world of free choice, it is all the more important to be clear and single-minded in pursuing the object of the game.

B. Influencing attitudes about yourself

How you write can determine how you rate! It can be even more important than how you look, or speak, or handle yourself in meetings and one-on-one conversations. Your writing travels up and down the corporate ladder, well beyond the bounds of your personal contacts, and carries with it a demonstration of who you are, how you work, and how you think.

Do not feel bashful about targeting your writing to reflect your personal attitudes and attributes. If you are good, your company wants to know it, and the sooner the better. Success depends on identifying and utilizing the strengths and capabilities of their people. If you hide your light under a bushel basket, you are hurting the company as much as you are hurting yourself.

What are the characteristics you want your writing to reflect? It depends on who you are and what your actual performance can live up to. Some of the positive attitudes which your writing can reflect are:

Strength

Wisdom

Leadership

Energy

Clarity

Prudence

Foresight

Creativity

Judgment

Thoroughness

How your writing can communicate these kinds of messages is discussed in the section on Style. But it is an essential that your communication include some kind of message about *you*.

III. IDENTIFYING THE BENEFITS

Organize your entire presentation around
reader benefits, explicit and implicit.

Identify the central benefit and structure your
writing around it.

If there is no benefit promised, why should
anybody bother to start reading?

If no benefit is delivered in the first paragraph, why read the second?

Reader interest is like the classic definition of
gratitude—it is based on a lively expectation of benefits to come.

And that expectation is based on benefits re-
ceived. Stop feeding benefits and your
reader interest is gone.

Boredom is based on your reader's perception
that "there is nothing in this for me."

But don't be confused. "Good news" is not the
only kind of benefit.

27

For instance, information can be a benefit to your reader if it:

Gives confidence that the situation is controlled or controllable.

Tells what the real-world problems and options are.

Eliminates surprises and uncertainty.

Communicates the actions you have taken and plan to take, and the personal qualities you are demonstrating by your actions and plan.

Of course, good news is always welcome. If you have identified or uncovered an opportunity, solved a problem, disposed of a worry, that is a self-evident benefit.

But bad news can be a benefit too. It is a benefit to tell somebody that their house is on fire if you thereby prevent them from being burned in their bed. The one thing management hates most is being surprised by bad news; it is always a benefit to feel confident you know the worst!

You must be careful to identify and label something as a benefit only if your reader perceives it as such.

But whether or not you label it as a benefit, the benefit should be present in each paragraph *implicitly*. You benefit the reader because it contains something he knows he needs to know.

IV. GET TO THE POINT

Get there immediately!

This is the biggest benefit your writing can confer, whether it is directed downward, upward, or sideways.

A. Downward

Your subordinates have one basic question in mind as they pick up your communication, "What do they want me to *do?*" So tell them!

1. The first sentence may be the only thing they read, or the only thing they remember. Make sure, therefore, that it delivers the message.

2. From years of newspaper reading, people are trained to expect the most *important* information in the headline. Whatever you put first in place, they will assume is first in importance.

3. By coming directly to the point, you help to fortify your own image as a clear, decisive leader (within your given area of authority).

Only after you have clearly established your main point should you get into the subordinate issues, e.g., **why** you should do such-and-such and **how** you should do such-and-such. Which comes first, the how or the why? You have to decide this on a case-by-case basis. Whichever question is uppermost in your reader's mind should receive priority of place.

This same principle applies, even if you are dealing with a situation where you want your reader to know something, rather than do something.

I am not suggesting that your attitude or tone of voice should seem abrupt, dictatorial, or cold. Quite the contrary: being clear and direct is a courtesy to your readers, a mark of respect. It indicates that you have taken the time to think through your communication, that you have taken it and them seriously.

B. Upward

Many of the same considerations apply, as well as some others.

1. Each member of your management, as they pick up your communication, has the same question in mind, "What *action* does this call for on my part?" The biggest benefit you can confer is to answer this question up front and not force your reader to burrow through your report trying to find it.

   Reasons and background are important

only insofar as they relate to proposed actions. Reasons and background can

(a) demonstrate that the proposed action will work, i.e., is viable,

(b) demonstrate that it is preferable to other available options,

(c) equip the reader to reach an independent judgment, which might be different from any of the options considered by the writer.

So reasons and background have an important place in many upward communications—but not at the top.

2. Your audience is made up of busy people. They have much to read and never enough time to read it all and think about it all. The more quickly your message can be grasped and acted on, the more valuable your contribution.

3. Your own image is being shaped every time you write. If you persist in writing in the form of a detective story—with the answer on the last page—you run the risk of producing reactions like:

"Trying to duck responsibility . . . trying to get me to make the decision for him [her]."
"Wasting my time telling me a lot of things I know better than she[he] does."

> "Overwhelmed by detail . . . does not know how to organize and activate . . . not material for promotion."

The myth is wrong. The Ancient Greeks did not kill the messenger who brought bad news. They killed the messenger who when asked "Who won?" replied, "First, let me give you a little background. There was this Queen named Helen, see . . . the best looking woman in the whole Mediterranean. And there was this King . . ."

C. Sideways

Any communication in which no power flows in either direction—from writer to reader or vice versa—depends on voluntary maintenance of interests. So if your very first sentence isn't involving, your second sentence may never be read.

This does not mean that your opening sentence should be crass, naked, cold—without charm, courtesy, or goodwill. On the contrary it means that you should not waste time and space "clearing your throat." Here are some examples of what not to do.

> "I am writing to tell you of our new policy with respect to past-due payments."

> *(I can see that you are writing—but not why. How does your new policy affect me. . . . Or does it?)*

> "For some time now customers have been
> asking us whether we could make next-
> day shipment in cases of real
> emergency."

> **("Once upon a time there were three
> bears . . ." Are you telling me a story
> or do you have some news for me. And
> is it good or bad?)**

I could go on ad infinitum. Your own mail is
full of thousands of examples of letters,
brochures, and proposals that fail to command
your immediate interest and attention because
the writer paid insufficient attention to this vital
point.

For any situation there are dozens of scores of
"right" ways of solving this problem. I will give
one example, not because it is the best, but
because it is the easiest for both of us at this
moment. Go back and read the first two paragraphs of this book, and analyze what I at-
tempted to communicate. . . .

My message to you:

1. This book is going to be easy to read, maybe
   even fun.

2. The writer is a pro.

3. The book is written for big leaguers.

To accomplish this communication, I had to:

1. First, define these as my primary strategic objectives to convincing you to read or buy this book.

2. Second, find the language and image that would fit my objectives, suit my tactics to match my strategy.

I have used this example to reemphasize that coming to the point does not mean being crude or blunt. It means making your very first sentence move you in the direction you want to go.

TACTICS

Up to now we have been dealing with a rather structured situation. There is usually only *one* strategy that is right for the occasion, and the problem is to find it.

But there are hundreds of right ways of writing what you need to write, and the problem is to choose one of them.

My object is not to help you get *the* right answer. It is to help you get *a* right answer.

Similarly, when you critique the writing of people who report to you, I urge you to remember: there are hundreds of right ways of writing something. (But there are millions of wrong ways.)

I. THE TOOLS OF THE WRITING TRADE

There are four basic elements, each of which serves a different purpose.

The Composition: This is the skeleton, to which are attached the muscles, inside which are housed vital organs. As with a human being, we should be able to see the bones of your outline underneath the flesh and blood of your report. When we can see the structure under the flesh, it makes us feel that the entire organism is articulated, has the power of purposeful motion, is not an amorphous blob like a jelly fish floating in the water.

The Paragraph: This is the unit that contains a single concept, properly described. Usually the first sentence, the topic sentence, summarizes the content of the paragraph. Indented subparagraphs can be used if the paragraph becomes lengthy or complicated.

The Sentence: This is the vehicle to communicate a single fact, idea, or relationship that contributes to a concept. Sentences can be long or short—simple, compound, complex, or compound-complex.

The two essential things to remember are:

(1) that sentences be easy to read and understand, and
(2) that their structure be varied to achieve an inviting
paragraph that maintains interest.

Very often in business writing you will find the first
sentence of each paragraph underlined or boldfaced.
This provides a great convenience to the busy reader
who can skip from topic sentence to topic sentence
reading entire paragraphs only when the topic sentence
is not evident. Be careful about using any structure that
can become monotonous and can allow the reader to fall
into habits of inattention.

<u>The Words:</u> The words you choose communicate not
only what you say, but also what kind of person you are,
who you think your readers are, and what kind of
relationship you are seeking to establish with them.

From this brief overview let us move to a specific
examination of how to use these four tools.

A. The Composition

1. Organize your outline by listing the benefits.

> Put the benefit most important to your
> reader first.

> List the other benefits in descending order
> of importance.

> Before you start to explain any of them,
> list all the benefits.

For purposes of your outline your concept of a benefit can be broadly construed.

Here are some examples of possible benefits:

A course of action to be taken by you, your superior, your subordinate, or your suppliers

The identification of a problem, a non-problem, or an opportunity or achievement

A product or service that meets the needs of a customer or company

But be sure to think this through in your own mind. For example:

A new product is *not* a benefit. What the new product *does* is a benefit.

A new opportunity is not a benefit.

Taking advantage of the opportunity will be a benefit.

A plan to solve a problem is not a benefit. Carrying out the plan is a benefit.

2. Allow your reader to understand the structure of your presentation, so he(she) can find what he is looking for and skip what he already knows and understands.

One of the great advantages of the written over the oral presentation is the active role the reader can play. The reader has the freedom to skip, reread, underline, annotate. (By contrast, the audience to an oral presentation is perforce passive. Nothing they can do will speed the speaker up, slow him down, change his emphasis.) You want the reader to feel actively involved—to sit on the edge of his chair, pencil in hand, as he reads your communication. If he reads right through your communication without skipping, that is best. It is a tribute to the strength and logic of your argument and the thrust and momentum of your style. But many readers' minds work in a unique way, making original leaps and associations. Let it be easy for this kind of reader to find what he is looking for.

3. Organize the presentation of your supporting argument with the following factors in mind.

Classify your material into main points, subpoints, and (if necessary) sub-sub points.

There are various kinds of subpoints:

a. Those that subdivide the main point into various classifications. (This is the structure I am using right now.)

b. Those that show some of the causes or reasons for the main point.

    c. Those that show some of the consequences or implication of the main point.

Include material which you think is significant—or which your reader will think significant.

If it is necessary to include material such as blind alleys you have explored or details of how you did what you did, try to insert them as footnotes or attachments so they will not interrupt the flow.

4. When it comes time to transform your outline into a piece of writing:

    a. Prepare a simple topic sentence that states each point or subpoint.

    b. Indent paragraphs containing subpoints.

    c. Underline topic sentences, if it is not contrary to the corporate style.

B. The Paragraph

The paragraph is like a biological cell, containing one nucleus, one single concept. That concept may be a fact, a condition, a relationship, a trend, or a tendency. So there may be a number of different things or ideas contained in the paragraph. But the guiding principle is that they can all be wrapped up in a cohesive, flowing thought.

The previous paragraph illustrates that point. Its one cohesive thought being that paragraphs have one cohesive thought.

And the *two* previous paragraphs illustrate three important points:

1. The length of each paragraph should be determined by its subject matter. But that is not the whole story. . . .

2. Paragraphs in sequence should not all be the same length. You should have a nice mix—some longer, some shorter—to maintain an attractive variety. There is no rule, thank goodness. You just have to sensitize yourself.

3. Finally no paragraph should look uninvitingly long. If it runs over about one hundred twenty-five words, it will seem intimidating no matter well written.

   The above section illustrates how to subdivide and indent paragraphs for easier reading and understanding.

   Finally these paragraphs illustrate perhaps the most important principle of all:

THRUST.

That is, give momentum to your writing and you will propel your reader forward to the next paragraph, and the next, and the next.

You maintain thrust by giving the reader a benefit in every paragraph. Such a benefit might be:

A fact relevant to the issue

An alternative idea

An assurance that all facets of the subject have been considered

But if there is no benefit in the previous
paragraph, why should the reader expect one
in the next? That is how you lose your
readership. *If you cannot put a benefit in,
take the paragraph out.*

If there is an easy, logical way of connect-
ing the new paragraph to the old one, that
helps to maintain thrust, but if there is not,
do not agonize over it. The problem of
transitions is the most troublesome one faced
by professional—even best-selling—writers.
Here are a few points that might help:

1. If you can build in a carryover at the end
   of your previous paragraph (as we just
   did) that helps.

2. If you have several paragraphs to write on
   a subject and they have no apparent
   connection with each other, label them 1,
   2, 3. (Again, as we are doing now.)

3. If you can, connect paragraphs with words such as, *therefore, hence, as expected, surprisingly, elsewhere, contrariwise.* They will contribute to a sense of coherence. Of course, be sure there is some justification for the connective you use.

4. If no graceful and logical transition suggests itself, simply move ahead. Do not lose momentum and thrust trying to contrive a connection. You can always go back and polish your writing later.

C. The Sentence

1. Often a paragraph will be only one sentence long. That is fine. There is an old saying, "Least said, most remembered."

2. Of course, sentences can be long or short. They can be simple, compound, complex, or compound-complex. The important thing is that they should vary in length and structure. Simple sentences (like this one) are the strongest and clearest. But a succession of simple sentences, all constructed in the same way, is monotonous, sometimes to the point of being almost hypnotic. The effect is like listening to a speaker who never changes his tone of voice or expression. Use short powerful sentences to drive home your points. Use longer, more graceful sentences to set up the reader for the clincher.

3. In grammar the basic rule is that every sentence have a subject (noun or pronoun) and a predicate (verb or verb and its object).

   In plain English this means "Who did what to whom."

   Make sure that your sentences always make this meaning clear and easy to follow. If the meaning is unclear, try moving your noun and verb closer together.

4. There are two ways of describing a condition or event. These are called active and passive.

We raised our prices.	ACTIVE
Our prices went up.	PASSIVE
We reduced our prices.	ACTIVE
Our prices were reduced.	PASSIVE
I made a mistake.	ACTIVE
A mistake was made.	PASSIVE
I had a good idea.	ACTIVE
A good idea came to mind.	PASSIVE

As you can see, the active voice gives a sharp, clear picture. Use it to highlight good news, strong points.

The passive voice takes the cutting edge off everything. People do not do things;

events simply happen. There are no bad guys, only bad actions. There are no heroes, only modest observers. The passive voice is the voice to use when you want to soften the spotlight, stay out of the limelight, help a situation to go away quietly.

Carrying the passive voice to its logical conclusion, in a given situation you could write:

A price rise occurred.

instead of

Our prices went up.

The passive voice is the ultimate cop out.

The use of the passive in business communications has become customary in many circles. (The previous sentence is a perfect example of the passive voice in action: nobody *did* anything, it just happened.) Whenever and wherever you can use the active voice without creating the impression that you are shouting in church, do so.

5. Learn to vary sentence structure, as well as the length of sentences. Do not start each the same way. For instance, both the previous sentences started with an order, an imperative. If there had been a third sentence also starting with an order, you might begin to feel pushed around. Why not interject a sentence in question form, for the sake of

interest and variety? (We just did!) There is no rule or formula for how to vary your sentence structure: you just have to develop your own awareness of the importance of doing so.

6. Whenever possible a sentence should be structured in terms of what the reader gets, rather than in terms of what the writer did. This must be applied with judgment. An example follows.

> If you are writing a report to management about what you did or plan to do, tell them that. Do not agonize over how to phrase your plans or actions in terms of benefits to the reader. If the actions worked or the plans make sense, that is the benefit your reader is looking for.

7. You may find yourself having to choose between observing the rules of grammar and the overriding need to communicate simply and effectively.

   Take the rule that you must never end a sentence with a preposition. Winston Churchill proclaimed:

> "This is the kind of nonsense up
> with which I do not intend to put."

If you have to choose between such slavish

adherence to a rule of grammar or violation of the rule for the sake of being clear and colloquial—choose neither! Rewrite the sentence! Churchill's statement now reads:

> "This is nonsense! I do not intend to
> put up with it!"

The reason you do not violate rules of grammar is that you are sure to find, within almost any business organization, some people who feel that such a violation betrays not only a deficient education, but a looseness with respect to rules in general.

If you are writing for people outside the organization, an entirely different set of considerations apply. If you want to be perceived as one of them, you use the kind of grammar that they use and feel comfortable with.

For instance, the marketers of Winston cigarettes quite cheerfully accepted the ridicule that the purists directed at their slogan, "Winston Tastes Good Like a Cigarette Should." They had asked themselves the question, "Would you rather do business with the people who say *like* or the people who say *as*? And the answer was overwhelmingly against grammatical propriety. So Winston by the use of a single word was able to communicate to the far larger audience who employ the colloquial, "We are talking to you. We are your kind of product."

D. The Words

You use words not only to communicate meaning but also feeling, not only to describe what you did but also to communicate the kind of person you are, for example, your values, your culture, your personality.

The quickest way to establish a bond with your reader is to speak the same language, to use the same kind of words in the same way that the reader would.

Here are some pointers that may help you.

1. Everybody uses everyday language in most of their everyday life. It is your reader's first language, the one they feel most comfortable with, the one they understand without effort. So use it as much as you can. When you write, use your normal speech and tone of voice. Do not get highfalutin or literal just because you are putting it on paper.

2. Technical, scientific, and professional words and language have several advantages:

   a. A single technical word can express a complex fact or relationship that would require a mouthful of common words to define. It saves time and space.

   b. Technical words have precise meanings; nontechnical synonyms often do not mean quite the same thing.

    c. Technical words—buzz words—establish a bond between reader and writer. You speak the same language, you have established your credentials.

3. But there are situations where buzz words and technical language are disadvantages.

    a. As your communication goes further up or down the corporate ladder, it reaches people who are increasingly less familiar or less comfortable with your technical language.

    b. There are many technical words that people know the meaning of, but only after they stop to think about it. Use of such words with these people does not block communication, but it slows it down, destroying the thrust and momentum you are striving for.

    c. And there are always people who will feel that the officious use of technical language is a mark of pushiness, snobbism, technical elitism, or phoniness.

4. You have to strike a balance between the conflicting forces, based on your sensitivity to the needs of your readers and the way they talk and think. (That is one reason why we placed the absolute number one priority

in the entire writing process on understanding your readers.) Here are some suggestions that apply in many—but not all—cases.

a. Use as few technical words as possible.

b. When you use a technical word for the first time, define it. (Unless this could be an insult to your readers.)

c. Try not to use several technical words in the same sentence. Introduce them one at a time.

Everything we have said about technical language applies equally to the use of acronyms. Some examples follow.

POP for Point of Purchase

DOA for Dead on Arrival

GATT for General Agreement on Taxes and Tariffs

As long as everybody understands what the acronym means, you save time and space by using it. But if some of your readers have to stop and puzzle out the meaning, it is counterproductive.

5. Try to use words that represent real things that can be touched, seen, felt, tasted, smelt —real actions that can be seen happening.

Words like these do more than reach the mind; they hit you in the belly. Your remember them because you *feel* them.

Concrete nouns, representing real things, instead of abstract nouns, representing ideas, attributes, forces, relationships, feelings, are most effective.

Concrete	*Abstract*
money	cash flow
work	employment
wood	forest products
air	circumambient atmosphere
people	personnel
house	residence
shoes	footwear
food	nutrition

Try to get a feeling for the difference between words with Anglo-Saxon roots and words with Latin or Greek roots. Going back to the days when the English language was being formed after the Norman Conquest, all the words for the common side of life came from Anglo-Saxon.

Nouns like
>blood, bread, house, hand, foot, shoe.

Verbs like
>eat, drink, sleep, swim, hunt, cook.

All the elegant words for the elegant things done by lords and ladies, abbots and bishops, came from the Latin roots of the French language. Words rooted in Latin or Greek tend to be more precise—more sophisticated—more abstract. Science and technology tend to use a Latin-based vocabulary, because they are dealing with processes or relationships, not things. If you use too much Latin and Greek-rooted language, your writing will sound like Little Lord Fauntleroy, and your readers will want to kick you in the pants. (That is an Anglo-Saxon expression.)

6. Adjectives modify nouns, and adverbs modify verbs, and you should try to use as few of them as possible. If you use the *right* noun and verb, you may not need the modifiers. Some examples:

Noun   Verb   Adverb

Instead of: "Prices went up very fast."

Noun   Verb

Use: "Prices rocketed."

Noun   Verb

Instead of: "Labor relations became
Adverbial phrase
more tense"

Noun   Verb

Use: "Labor tensions tautened."

If you can change a verb instead of adding an adjective, you add color and movement to your writing. That is because verbs deal with *actions*, while adjectives or adverbs deal with condition or states of being.

7. Reject books that promise to help you to increase your vocabulary. The last thing your writing needs is words that you understand but your readers do not, or, even worse, words they think they understand, but really do not.

   Instead make better use of the words you already know. Choose the strong words, the clear words, the colorful words, the precise words that touch your meaning on the very tip of its nose.

8. Metaphor and simile are among the most effective ways of communicating, because they make it easy for the reader to visualize your message.

   The simile *compares* the familiar to the unfamiliar using the words *like* or *as*. An example is "My love is *like* a red red rose."

   A metaphor substitutes the familiar for the unfamiliar. An example is "We stand at the crossroads." (If this were a simile, it would read, "Our situation is *like* standing at the crossroads.")

   Obviously, metaphors are stronger and shorter than similes, but they can be tricky to handle. Mixed or overly colorful metaphors sometimes distract attention from the point you want to make.

   How and when to use metaphors and similes? Here are some do's and don't's.

DO USE

To dramatize importance

"We are fighting for our lives."

To facilitate understanding

"If we want to stay in this game, we have to put another chip into the pot."

To establish mood

"Only three more weeks to keep pitching the sales competition. As Yogi says, 'It is never over til it's over!'"

DO NOT USE

To explain the self-evident when your figure of speech will stand out "like a sore thumb" as fancy-pants writing. Stay within the kind of language and imagery your audience is used to seeing in the kind of communication you are writing. If you are calling for extra effort, do not say, "Ask not what your company can do for you. Ask what you can do for your company."

When your metaphor or simile is mixed or confused.

"This extra commission is a chance for all you tigers to go out there and feather your nests."

9. Analogy carries metaphor or simile a long step further forward. It enables your reader to understand a new concept, new situation, new product by comparing it with a familiar one.

For example, "Knowledge is to the mind as light is to the eye."

Perhaps the most famous of analogies is the story of Sir Isaac Newton and the falling apple, which illuminated for Newton the principle of universal gravitation. Analogy is a powerful tool for discovering and learning, as well as communicating. Skill in the discovery of analogous situations is a hallmark of creativity.

II. STYLE

Putting them all together—your structure, paragraphs, sentences, words, and metaphors—the combination is your style. And style in writing for business is just as tricky as style in dressing for business.

On the one hand it is essential that you are sensitive to the corporate culture: the way things are done, the degree to which individual variation is permissible, and the degree to which individuality is encouraged. On the other hand, it is important both to you and to the company:

> That your message get through, clearly, easily, unambiguously

> That your personal qualities and attributes also be communicated, so that your status and future in the company can be influenced appropriately.

How you thread your way through this minefield has got to be a reflection of your *own* personality and career strategy. You cannot successfully write like somebody else any more than you speak like somebody else.

But here's one suggestion: focus your attention on the facts—on the situation—not on yourself. If you use colorful words, images, or metaphors to express something, the effect on the reader should be:

Not: "Wow! That's great writing!"

Instead: "Gosh! Now I understand!"

or "Wow! That really calls for action!"

The kind of good writing you should strive for is like a pair of good glasses; they help the reader to see the object more clearly. If the reader is conscious of the glasses instead of the object, there is probably a thumbprint on the glasses. Tone it down, get closer to your meaning and the corporate culture.

III. PROCRASTINATION AND "WRITER'S BLOCK"

The more you have at stake in the piece you are writing, and the more respect you gain for the art of writing, the more likely you are to develop stage fright when it comes time to begin. Here are some suggestions that work.

1. Do not think of yourself as sitting down to do the complete piece. Only think of working on the first draft.

2. Before you write anything, prepare your outline. Think through the strategic issues: who your audience is, what your objectives are, what are your most important reader benefits. If you can write topic sentences for each point in the outline, fine. If not, just label the points so you will know the ground you intend to cover.

3. It is best to start writing from the top, but if you are stuck for the magic opening words, start somewhere else—anywhere else, just so you get going. Write fast. Let the juices flow freely. If what you write does not quite follow the outline, to hell with the outline. If you find yourself writing something that you would have never thought of before, let it stay in. That's creativity.

4. Any time you come to a place where you

need tables, statistics, or quotations, do not stop to look for them. Find them later.

5. When you get stuck for a word or phrase, do not sit there staring at the page.

    a. Try going back a couple of sentences. Approach your problem in a slightly different way, like a horse backing off before crossing a stony brook.

    b. If that does not work, drop it temporarily and attack your piece somewhere else.

    ABOVE ALL, KEEP GOING!

6. If you find you are not able to finish the first draft in one sitting, do not force yourself to continue writing until you are written out. If you do, you may face the problem of writer's block all over again when you resume.

    Instead stop in the middle of a sentence—in the middle of a paragraph—where it is perfectly obvious to you what you are going to say next. Then when it is time to resume your writing, you can do it easily. You do not have to rev up your motor; you can just take off the brake and roll away.

7. Try to get a clear idea of what you are going to say, but not too tight an idea of how you are going to say it. You will be surprised to

find out how many sentences that seem great when you think about them or say them to yourself do not look quite right when you put them down on paper. Often the tone of voice is not what you want, maybe too dramatic or too pontifical or too contentious. If this happens, there is a great temptation to fuss around fixing that one sentence, instead of letting the work start flowing.

Once you have started to work,

LET YOUR FINGERS DO THE WRITING!

Self-criticism and rewriting comes later.

8. Sometimes writers get stage fright because as they start to write they know what they want to say, but they are not quite comfortable with their tone of voice. They write a couple of sentences and then pause in embarrassed self-doubt. "Does that sound too pushy? Too mousy? Am I patronizing my readers? Do I communicate a sense of confidence or over-confidence?"

This underlines the basic importance of the second fundamental of writing:

KNOW YOUR OBJECTIVES.

As we have already said, this includes defining your own relationship to what you are reporting or recommending or trying to sell.

You have to develop a very sure sense of how you are perceived and how you want to be perceived. We can't solve this problem for you, all we can do is to make you aware of the necessity of your facing it and solving it.

IV. REWRITING AND CUTTING

Rewriting is what makes good writing good, and cutting is the most important part of rewriting.

1. All good writers rewrite. They do not expect to get it right the first time. They only expect to get it on paper the first time.

2. Once you have written something on a piece of paper, that piece of paper is no longer you, that piece of paper is it. It becomes an object—something you can look at objectively. Keep what is good, fix what is not, or crumple it up and make a fresh start.

   You must not feel that when you crumple up that piece of paper, you have discarded a piece of yourself. What you have done is to state, "I can do this better and I will."

3. When somebody else criticizes something you have written, you have to assume the same attitude. They are not criticizing the writer, they are criticizing what is written.

4. So concentrate first on the strategic issues, as we have defined them here.

    Who are you writing to?

    What are you trying to accomplish?

    What is the benefit to your reader?

    What is the bottom line?

    What is the structure of your argument?

    Use what you have learned here as a checklist at rewrite time, just like when your automobile goes back to the dealer for its fifty-thousand-mile overhaul.

    If it takes a major restructuring to get the strategic issues right, take the time to do it, even if it is a rush job and you have to sacrifice correcting the tactical issues.

5. If there is a word, sentence, or paragraph that does not seem quite right, before you spend a lot of time trying to change it, see if you cannot cut it out entirely.

    It is surprising how much pace, drive, and clarity you can achieve by stripping away decorative or distracting non-essentials. When you strip away the fat, the skeleton— the essential structure—becomes visible.

6. Always keep a clean copy of your original draft when you are working on your rewrite.

You may change your mind as you work and want to refer to the original.

If you are working with typed or handwritten copy, keep a clean Xerox. If you are working on a word processor, be sure you have a hard copy of the original. If you can have a duplicate original on the disc, that is better—and safer.

7. Working on hard copy, I use a set of colored felt-tipped pens. The first time I go over a draft I use one color, and each succeeding time a different color.

So instead of my copy getting to look dirtier and more disgusting as I work on it, it gets to look more and more colorful. That keeps up my spirits as I keep my nose on the rewriting grindstone.

V. THE WRAP UP

After you have finished with the rewrite, you may feel the need for a summary that pulls the whole piece together.

My suggestion is after you have written the summary *put it at the beginning instead of the end.*

Of course, if you are writing a sideways business communication, you have an additional problem: to translate the motivation and communication you have been building up into action. If you have followed our advice and implanted the necessity for action from the very beginning, this should not be a major problem. But if you find that your call to action does not flow naturally out of the thrust of your whole composition, take the time to go back and plant the necessary seeds in the early going. Do not let your "closing" appear as an afterthought or intrusion.

11 KEYS TO WRITING

1. Visualize your audience.

2. Define your objectives.

3. What are the benefits?

4. Come to the point FAST.

5. Make an outline.

6. Write topic sentences.

7. A benefit in every paragraph.

8. Write fast.

9. Use plain words.

10. Rewrite until it is right.

11. Cutting is better than changing.

APPENDIX

BEFORE REWRITING—AND AFTER

There are thousands of wrong ways of writing a business communication—following are a few random examples.

As an exercise I suggest that you (1) write your own criticism of each from a *strategic* point of view. (2) Then rewrite the communication to implement your criticism; to keep things simple, use the wording of the original communication insofar as possible. (3) Then compare what you did with my suggestions, which begin on page 74. (Yours may be *better* than mine. I hope they are! Remember there are hundreds of right tactics for every strategy.)

EXAMPLES

LETTER 1

Market Research Company
R & D Boulevard
Commerce, U.S.A.

Dear Linda:

Enclosed is a copy of the questionnaire we used on the callbacks for the Jams/Jellies Group participants. As we discussed, we are asking for children's reactions on an open-ended basis rather than structured. The reason for this was to avoid respondents voicing their own impressions, which you are more likely to get if the questions are structured. In using an open-ended format we can at least determine whether the children made any comments, and if they did, then determine what they were.

With respect to the flavors each respondent will be asked to evaluate up to four flavors. Since there are no records indicating which flavors were given to which people, we had to use one standard questionnaire pre-listing *all* possible flavors. This will make your client's hand tab a rather tedious procedure.

With the questionnaire having to be revised to accommodate all possible flavors, we will not be able to start interviewing until Friday the 25th. We still expect to be finished by Wednesday the 30th.

Very truly yours,

Research Director

LETTER 2

The Future Group
Bountiful, U.S.A.

Dear Group Administrator:

The 198X United States Sports & Fitness
Show opens October 12, 13, and 14 at the (some
place) Civic Center Exhibition Hall.

Allworthy Health Helpers is sponsoring the
show in cooperation with the University of Some
Place Health Center and Monitor Productions.
This is a brand new endeavor and one which we
think you will find exciting.

We understand your specific interest in
topics such as Corporate Fitness and Health
Promotion because we know companies and indi-
viduals are facing increased costs in the areas
of health care. We believe the workshops, demonstrations, and the individual booth exhibits
can help you find ways to help contain costs at
your company.

Friday, October 12 has been designated Cor-
poration Day. Five specially designed workshops will be presented on Employee Health and
Fitness. The University of Some Place Health
Center is coordinating the workshops and has
scheduled nationally known speakers for each.
In addition, demonstration areas will be
operating throughout the show. Agendas for the
workshops and demonstrations during all three
days are enclosed.

There are four ways in which your company
can be involved in the show.

  1. You can purchase tickets. Tickets for the
     United States Sports & Fitness Show are
     available at the Civic Center box office.
     Prices are $4 for adults and $2 for chil-

dren sixteen years of age and younger. Key
staff members involved with your employee
benefit area are urged to attend.
Blocks of tickets may be purchased for employees. Ticket discounts are available
for groups of twenty-five or more. For
discount ticket information, contact Ms.
Ticketlady, 1 Civic Center Plaza, Some
Place (XXX/YYY-ZZZ).

2. Corporations such as Good Guys, Nice Guys,
   Good Chaps, and others have purchased
   booth space to explain their programs to
   the public. Some booth space is still
   available. If your company has a product,
   service, or program that is appropriate,
   please consider a booth.

3. Corporations such as Some Company and
   Another One are sponsoring one or more of
   the University of Some Place demonstration
   areas. Such sponsorships help to defray
   part or all of the costs involved in pre-
   senting these state-of-the-art fitness
   demonstrations. Sponsorship provides good
   public exposure for your company and helps
   with a good cause. Information on booth
   rentals and demonstration sponsorships
   can be obtained from Miss Nicelady,
   Monitor Productions, City Place, Some
   Place (AAA/BBB-CCCC).

4. Help us to publicize the Bill Rodgers 10-K
   Classic Road Race. The race through downtown Some Place will begin at 10 A.M. at
   the Some Place Civic Center. The first
   1,000 runners will be given commemorative
   T-shirts.
   If there are runners in your organization
   who would like to participate, registration forms are available through the YMCA,
   160 Some Street, Some Place. One form is
   included here. Early registration will

take place the morning of the race from
7:30 to 9:00 A.M. Prizes will be awarded.
You will also be able to meet and listen to
a variety of personalities including Bill Rodgers, Emmy Award—winning news reporter Miss
Talkwell, and others.
We are confident that you, your company,
and your employees will enjoy the 198X United
States Sports & Fitness Show. We invite each of
you to stop at our booth on the exhibition
floor.
Friday October 12 the show will open at noon
and run to 10:00 P.M. On Saturday the show hours
are 10:00 A.M. to 10:00 P.M. On Sunday the show
will open at noon after the Bill Rodgers 10—K
Classic Road Race. The show will close at 6:00
P.M.

Sincerely,

Director of Corporate Communications

MY CRITIQUE

LETTER 1

The benefits to the reader of this letter are:
1. Reassurance that the report will be delivered on
    time.
2. Clarification of what it will contain, based on recent
    changes.
3. Warning of possible problems in hand-tabbing that
    must be prepared for.

But the original letter has no visible structure, benefit, or organization.

Without changing any words, the following rewrite

enables the reader to more easily grasp the message and respond appropriately. Ultimately the letter should help to maintain a feeling of satisfaction with the service being provided.

LETTER 2

This letter has a very important primary benefit to offer—ways of reducing the cost of health-care.

It also has other benefits: opportunities for concerned employees to hear nationally known speakers and see demonstrations as well as a medium for displaying products, services, and programs.

But the benefits are obscured in a mass of unorganized and redundant verbiage. For example, the whole of paragraph two and all of paragraph three but the last twelve words can—and should—be eliminated.

If I were doing this, I would write a very short letter saying:

```
   On October 12 through 14 you have a special
opportunity to find new ways to help contain
health care costs at your company.
   The great event is the 198X U.S. Sports &
Fitness Show.
   There will be workshops, exhibits, demon-
strations, five nationally known authorities
leading discussions and answering questions—
plus an opportunity for your company to explain
and exhibit your product or service.
   All the details are in the enclosed brochure.
Don't miss it!
                                     Sincerely
```

However, if the poor writer's boss told him to handle the whole thing in a letter, here's how he could have structured it more intelligently without changing any of the words or ideas.

REWRITE

LETTER 1

Market Research Company
R & D Boulevard
Commerce, U.S.A.

Dear Linda:

There will be no delay in completing the callback interviews on the Jams/Jellies Group participants, despite the changes that we agreed to make. The start of interviewing will be delayed until Friday the 25th, but we still expect to complete it on Wednesday the 30th.

Confirming our discussion, two types of changes will be made.

a. Children's reactions will be asked for on an open-ended basis instead of a struc-tured one. This will enable us to deter-mine whether children made any comments, and if so, what they were.

b. Each respondent will be asked to evaluate up to four flavors. The questionnaire, however, will pre-list all possible flavors. This is necessary because no records were kept indicating which flavors were given to which people. As a result, your client's hand tab will be a rather tedious procedure.

                                        Very truly yours,

LETTER 2

The Future Group
Bountiful, U.S.A.

Dear Group Administrator:

    The 198X United States Sports & Fitness
Show, which opens October 12, 13 and 14 at the
Some Place Civic Center Exhibition Hall, can
help you find ways to help contain health care
costs at your company.
    On Friday October 12 five workshops will be
presented on Employee Health and Fitness with
nationally known speakers for each. In addition, demonstration areas will be operating
throughout the show. Agendas for all three days
are enclosed.
    Here's how your company can benefit. . . .

  1. Key staff members involved with your em-
     ployee benefit area are urged to purchase
     tickets for the United States Sports &
     Fitness Show at the Civic Center box of-
     fice. $4.00 for adults and $2.00 for chil-
     dren sixteen years of age and younger.
     Blocks of tickets may be purchased. Dis-
     counts are available for groups of twenty-
     five or more. Contact Ms. Ticketlady, 1
     Civic Center Plaza, Some Place (AAA/
     BBB-CCCC).
  2. Join corporations such as Good Guys, Nice
     Guys, Good Chaps, and others and purchase
     booth space to explain your product, serv-
     ice, or program.
  3. Join corporations such as Some Company and
     Another One in sponsoring one or more of
     the University of Some State's state-of-
     the-art fitness demonstrations. Sponsor-

ship provides good public exposure for
your company and helps support a good
cause.
For information on booth rentals and demonstration sponsorships, call Ms.
Nicelady, Monitor Productions, City
Place, Some Place (XXX/YYY–ZZZZ).

4. Help us to publicize the Bill Rodgers 10–K
   Classic Road Race through downtown Some
   Place, beginning at 10 A.M. at the Some
   Place Civic Center. The first 1,000 runners will be given commemorative T–shirts,
   and prizes will be awarded.
   Runners in your organization can get registration forms through the YMCA, 160 Some
   Street, Some Place, or the morning of the
   race from 7:30 to 9:00 A.M. A sample form
   is enclosed.

You will also be able to meet in person Bill
Rodgers, Emmy Award–winning news reporter, Ms.
Talkwell, and other notable personalities.

We invite each of you to stop at our booth
on the exhibition floor.

Friday October 12 the show will be open from
noon to 10:00 P.M. On Saturday from 10:00 A.M.
to 10:00 P.M. On Sunday the show will open at
noon after the Bill Rodgers 10–K Classic Road
race, and close at 6:00 P.M.

Sincerely,

Director of Corporate Communications

INDEX